W9-BOO-058

basketball

a *flow*motion™ title

basketball

mark dunning

Sterling Publishing Co., Inc.
New York

Created and conceived by
Axis Publishing Limited
8c Accommodation Road
London NW11 8ED
www.axispublishing.co.uk

Creative Director: Siân Keogh
Managing Editor: Brian Burns
Design: Axis Design Editions
Project Editor: Conor Kilgallon
Production Manager: Sue Bayliss
Production Controller: Juliet Brown
Photographer: Mike Good

Library of Congress Cataloging-in-Publication Data
Available

10 9 8 7 6 5 4 3 2 1

Published in 2003 by Sterling Publishing Co., Inc.
387 Park Avenue South, New York, NY 10016
Text and images © Axis Publishing Limited 2003
Distributed in Canada by Sterling Publishing
c/o Canadian Manda Group,
One Atlantic Avenue, Suite 105
Toronto, Ontario, Canada, M6K 3E7

Every effort has been made to ensure that all the
information in this book is accurate. However, due to
differing conditions, and individual skills, the publisher
cannot be responsible for any injuries, losses, and other
damages which may result from the use of the
information in this book.

All rights reserved. No part of this book may be
reproduced in any form, by photostat, microfilm,
xerography, or any other means, or incorporated into any
retrieval system, electronic or mechanical, without the
written permission of the copyright owner.

ISBN 0–8069–9372–3

Printed by Star Standard (Pte) Limited

a *flowmotion*™ title

basketball

contents

introduction

The popularity of basketball is such that it now enjoys a truly global status, played and watched by an estimated 300 million people. This makes it second only to soccer in terms of level of participation and interest.

As well as grass-roots interest at amateur level, most countries now have national federations that organize not only professional leagues for men and women, but also formal competitive leagues for boys and girls of all ages.

National teams also compete at this global level and club teams contest world championships, as well as championships for European, Asian, African, and Pan American geographical areas. The most famous, wealthy, and hotly contested league in the world is run by the National Basketball Association (NBA) in the United States,

As well as the able-bodied "running" game, there is also a thriving wheelchair game that has its own world championships and other competitions which are run along the same lines as the able-bodied game.

Basketball is also one of the most popular and keenly contested Olympic sports, and the popularity of the original U.S. "Dream Team" in 1992 was a story that has become part of Olympic Games' legend.

the origins of the game

The game today has inevitably evolved and improved since its inception in 1891 in Springfield, Massachusetts, home now to the Basketball Hall of Fame. The man who created this immediately successful sport was the Canadian Dr. James

Balance, good footwork, and the ability to think and react quickly are prerequisites for basketball.

Naismith who had sought to find a team game suitable for indoor play during the harsh winter months of the northern United States. Drawing on an activity he had learned as a child, Naismith developed basketball's original 13 rules and, consequently, the game itself. However, Naismith regarded himself as a physical educator and academic and never sought to profit from his great invention. He received his greatest compliment in 1936 when basketball became an Olympic sport at the Berlin games. Naismith died in 1939.

The top professionals exhibit speed, agility, and athleticism each time they run onto the court. Aim to emulate them.

the game

Basketball as we know it now is a fast, dynamic sport played by great athletes who need to have the total fitness package in order to play the game successfully at the highest levels. However, it is as enjoyable as a recreational pastime as when played by serious professionals.

scoring and fouls

Basketball is usually played indoors by a team of five players and lasts for 40 minutes (international and NCAA rules) or 48 minutes (United States' NBA league rules). In both versions of the game, the total time is divided into four equal quarters with a 15-minute break at half-time. A whole basketball team, however, is comprised of 10 players (12 in the NBA), which allows for five (or seven NBA) substitutes to be used during the course of the game.

Basketball is almost unique in its high scoring system, which makes for exciting games and nail-biting pressure. The other feature of the scoring is that no game can be tied. So when scores are level, five-minute periods of overtime are played until one team wins.

The triple-threat position is the basic fundamental for all players upon receiving the basketball.

The basket itself is a bottomless net hanging off a metal ring, 18in (46cm) in diameter, and attached to a backboard 10ft (3.05m) above the floor. Each basket, or "field goal," scores two points, or three points if shot from behind a line nearly 24ft (7.3m) from the basket. Teams must attempt at shot within 24 seconds of getting the ball (NBA and FIBA rules); otherwise, it is handed over to the opposition.

Any player making illegal body contact with an opposing player is judged to have committed a foul; when this happens, the opposing team may be given possession of the ball, or an opposing player is awarded free throws at the basket from the foul line. Each made foul shot is worth one point. Players who exceed the foul limit (usually five, but six in the NBA) are disqualified from the game.

Scoring is affected by the rules governing fouls. Most contact that is deemed by the referees (of whom there are two in international play and three in the NBA) to be either deliberate or which places an opponent at a disadvantage is penalized by a personal foul being levied against the offending player. These fouls may result in the opposing team being given the ball or an opposing player being given free throws from the foul line. A player who accumulates five fouls (six in the NBA) is ejected from the game.

Unsportsmanlike and more serious offences are penalized by a "technical foul," often given for dissent and punishable by a free throw. Technical fouls can also be levied against coaches. A coach who gets two of these in a game is disqualified from the contest and must leave the court.

skills

As well as learning the rules, all players must master the basic skills of the game. The skills contained in this book are the individual techniques that form the basis of the game and are the ones that every player must acquire in order to be able to participate in the game effectively. The fundamentals of passing, dribbling, shooting, rebounding, and defensive footwork are covered. Professional players will spend countless hours refining these essentials, and serious players engage in a regular schedule of repetitive practice for several years working on the premise that "only perfect practice makes perfect" and that "perfect practice makes permanent." Only through this dedication can players compete to their full potential.

Work your way up and down the court, dribbling two basketballs and using alternate bounces.

the players and court

There are three main positions on the court: the guards, the forwards, and the centers. Usually the guards are the shorter members of the team, and the centers are the tallest. Centers tend to play nearer the basket while the more agile forwards and guards occupy areas of the court farther away from the basket area. The guards tend to do most of the ball handling and longer-range shooting, with the forwards typically driving to the basket from the wings. An NBA court is shown below (the FIBA international version uses a different 3-second area and 3-point line).

PLAYER POSITIONS

1. **point guard**
2. **shooting guard**
3. **small forward**
4. **power forward**
5. **centre**

COURT MARKINGS (NBA COURT)

a. **3-second area (the lane)**
b. **3-point line**
c. **free-throw line**
d. **side line**
e. **halfway line**
f. **end line**

point guard

This is the most important (and difficult) position on the court for offensive moves. The player must be unselfish, willing to pass to teammates, yet be able to score himself, set up offensive plays, work out, and do what is best for the team at any given moment, as well as being a great dribbler and a good shooter.

shooting guard

The shooting guard must be very agile and a good long-distance shooter. The player should be a good ball handler and be able to work quickly and accurately.

small forward

This position requires an unselfish player who can not only shoot from the outside but can also make good cuts to the basket with and without the ball. This player is usually a superior athlete.

power forward

The power forward must be a strong, athletic player who is a good rebounder and competent scorer from in and around the 3-second lane. This position demands a great deal of strength, meaning the player is often involved in the more physical side of the game, such as defense. Picking up offensive and defensive rebounds is another key skill.

center

The center is the most physical of all the five positions. Offensively, it requires an ability to score from close range while in close physical contact with the opposition's defense. Defensively, the center is the most important position, as he or she is the last line of defense against opponents driving toward the basket, so he or she must be able to block shots and be an excellent rebounder, turning defense into offense.

In the modern game, however, all players tend to be able to do almost everything and have become excellent all-rounders rather than specialists in one position only.

A one-on-one requires good awareness so that you can execute a pass to a teammate or move past your opponent without losing the ball.

equipment

You will need the right footwear and clothing to play basketball, though equipment is minimal. Basketball shoes, with the laces tied up properly, athletic socks, loose-fitting shorts, and a T-shirt are all you need.

Obviously, you will also need a ball. There are various basketballs available. The regulation full-size ball is a size 7, though a size 6 ball is used in the Women's National Basketball Association (WNBA) and by many female competitions. Also, the size 5 mini-basketball is often used in underage competitions. Balls come in a variety of materials, such as rubber, synthetic leather, and full-grain leather, and prices vary tremendously. Choose one to suit your age and size and make sure you look after it.

A basket and a ball are all you need to start practicing shooting some hoops in your backyard.

GOVERNING BODIES

- Basketball is organized on a worldwide scale by FIBA, the world governing body. This sets the international rules, including the size and shape of the court and its markings. As we have seen, the NBA in the United States sets slightly different rules, and the game is played on a slightly different-sized court.

- The NBA is considered to be the top league in the world and generates massive revenue from selling TV rights. The league itself comprises 29 teams, including such legendary names as the New York Knicks, the Boston Celtics, the LA Lakers, and the Chicago Bulls.
  Its megastar (and megarich) players have included Michael Jordan, Larry Bird, Kareem Abdul Jabaar, and Earvin "Magic" Johnson, as well as many others from the past. The female equivalent is the WNBA, which currently has 16 teams.

- Also in the United States, besides High School basketball, there is great interest in college basketball. The revenue-generating NCAA Division One college level has over 300 men's teams, not to mention the Division Two and Division Three programs, followed by an NAIA level for smaller schools. Finally, the Junior College system also runs a national competition.

streetball and urban cool

The popularity of the game worldwide is such that, in recent years, "streetball" has become a huge hit. Of course, most indoor basketball is played on sprung wooden floors, but the "blacktops" (the slang name for outdoor tarmac street courts) are used by ordinary people in urban neighborhood areas all over the world. There has always been a populist culture surrounding the outdoor basketball court. Many of the game's top players in the United States honed their skills on these courts, which are accessible to anyone wanting to shoot some hoops. In the United States, in particular, whole tournaments are played outdoors each summer and are hugely popular.

Another aspect of the game, and we have the NBA to thank for this, is the worldwide phenomenon of fashion, music, and "cool" that has become synonymous with the sport. Young people from all sorts of cultures are attracted by this, and indeed it is the combination of these aspects of the game that can bring together peoples of all races and nationalities united under one common theme—the great game of basketball.

The techniques shown in this book will give you a sound base on which to build your physical knowledge of the game. The various fundamental skills demonstrated are those that occur frequently in all basketball games at every level. They can be practiced and worked on alone and some do not even require a basket. Follow the flow of the pictures and try to copy them as you practice. Work hard, but above all, enjoy the game.

warming up

In basketball, not only must you constantly work on and practice your skills to ensure your technique is properly developed, but you must also pay significant attention to other areas such as body strength, cardiovascular fitness, and nutrition.

If you take these issues seriously—starting in your teenage years—your sporting ability will improve dramatically, not to mention your everyday health and vitality. Your coach or trainer should be able to advise you on the correct amounts of carbohydrates (for energy), protein (for muscle growth and repair), fats (preferably non-saturated), fiber (for healthy digestion), and vitamins and minerals for nutrition and the regulation of body systems. It is also extremely important to understand that you need to be in good physical health before undertaking vigorous sports such as basketball, and to this end you should consult your doctor to check your health before starting any training program.

This page and the ones that follow show some of the most common and effective warm-up and stretching exercises that should always be done prior to any vigorous physical activity. As a general rule, warm up for five to seven minutes with a slow-paced activity that doesn't involve any sharp

BUTT KICKS Work your way across the court in an exaggerated running motion, kicking your heels up behind you as high as you can.

CARIOCA Move across the court, crossing one foot in front of the other, while swiveling at the hips.

WALKING LUNGES Moving up and down the court, lunge foward, extending one leg and then the other. Maintain your balance at all times.

movements or changes of speed and direction. Then, follow the stretches outlined to prepare the muscles and joints for the vigorous movements experienced while playing or practicing basketball. The static stretches shown on pages 16–18, if done properly, are adequate to prepare you to play.

don't overstretch
Be disciplined in your approach to warming up and stretching. Never skip it, but also be aware that stretching should not hurt. Only stretch as far as feels comfortable. This will be enough to get a "stretch response," which you should maintain for around 20 to 30 seconds.

Do not "bounce" the muscle, just "squeeze" and hold in order to get a stretch response. Everyone is different, so get to know your own limitations and needs.

Another important thing to remember is never to play sport wearing jewelry. Take it off and store it in a safe, secure place before stepping onto the court.

stretching exercises

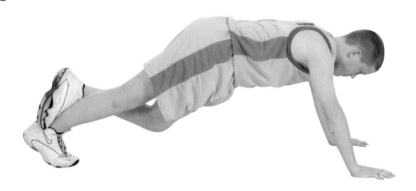

CALF STRETCH Straighten one leg, hooking the other over the heel. Push the heel of the straight leg down toward the ground. Feel the stretch in the calf muscle.

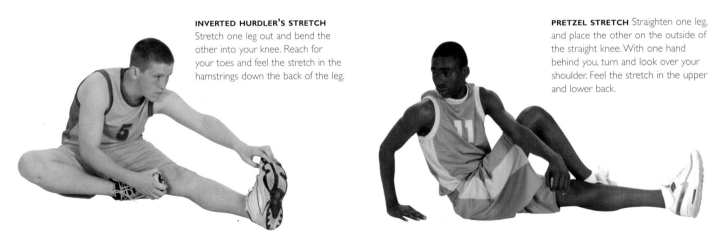

INVERTED HURDLER'S STRETCH Stretch one leg out and bend the other into your knee. Reach for your toes and feel the stretch in the hamstrings down the back of the leg.

PRETZEL STRETCH Straighten one leg, and place the other on the outside of the straight knee. With one hand behind you, turn and look over your shoulder. Feel the stretch in the upper and lower back.

BUTTERFLY STRETCH Put the soles of your feet together. Push your knees down toward the ground. Feel the stretch in your groin muscles.

QUADRICEPS STRETCH Lie on your side and pull one foot toward (but not directly against) your bottom. Feel the stretch in front of your thigh.

stretching exercises continued

HAMSTRING STRETCH
Lie on your back and extend one leg upward into the air. Grip this leg by the calf and pull it toward your chest, keeping the other foot on the floor. Feel the stretch in the hamstring down the back of the leg.

GLUTES STRETCH
Lie on your back and pull both knees into your chest. Feel the stretch in the gluteus maximus muscles in your buttocks.

LOWER BACK STRETCH
Lie on your back, arms out to your sides. Bring one knee across your body, keeping your shoulders in contact with the ground. Feel the stretch in the lower back.

go with the flow

The special Flowmotion images used in this book have been created to ensure that you see the whole movement—not just isolated highlights. Each of the image sequences flows across the page from left to right, demonstrating how the technique progresses, and the body and ball movements you should make to get the most out of each move. Each technique is also fully explained with step-by-step captions. Below this, another layer of information in the timeline breaks the move into its various stages, with instructions for the different actions you should carry out. The pause "button" symbol in the timeline indicates key moments in the sequence to which you should pay special attention.

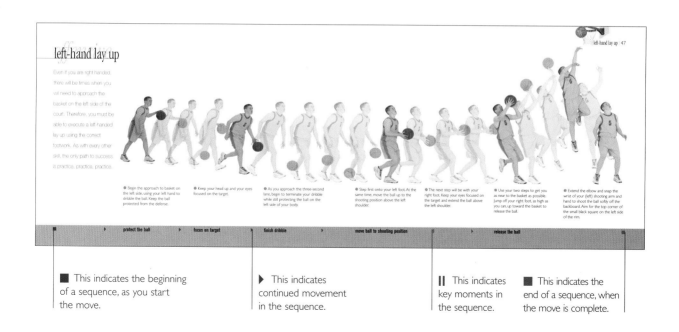

left-hand lay up : 47

left-hand lay up

Even if you are right-handed, there will be times when you will need to approach the basket on the left side of the court. Therefore, you must be able to execute a left-handed lay up using the correct footwork. As with every other skill, the only path to success is practice, practice, practice.

● Begin the approach to basket on the left side, using your left hand to dribble the ball. Keep the ball protected from the defense.

● Keep your head up and your eyes focused on the target.

● As you approach the three-second lane, begin to terminate your dribble while still protecting the ball on the left side of your body.

● Step first onto your left foot. At the same time, move the ball up to the shooting position above the left shoulder.

● The next step will be with your right foot. Keep your eyes focused on the target and extend the ball above the left shoulder.

● Use your two steps to get you as near to the basket as possible. Jump off your right foot, as high as you can, up toward the basket to release the ball.

● Extend the elbow and snap the wrist of your (left) shooting arm and hand to shoot the ball softly off the backboard. Aim for the top corner of the small black square on the left side of the rim.

■ ▶ protect the ball ▶ focus on target ◀ finish dribble ▶ move ball to shooting position ❚❚ ▶ release the ball ■■

■ This indicates the beginning of a sequence, as you start the move.

▶ This indicates continued movement in the sequence.

❚❚ This indicates key moments in the sequence.

■ This indicates the end of a sequence, when the move is complete.

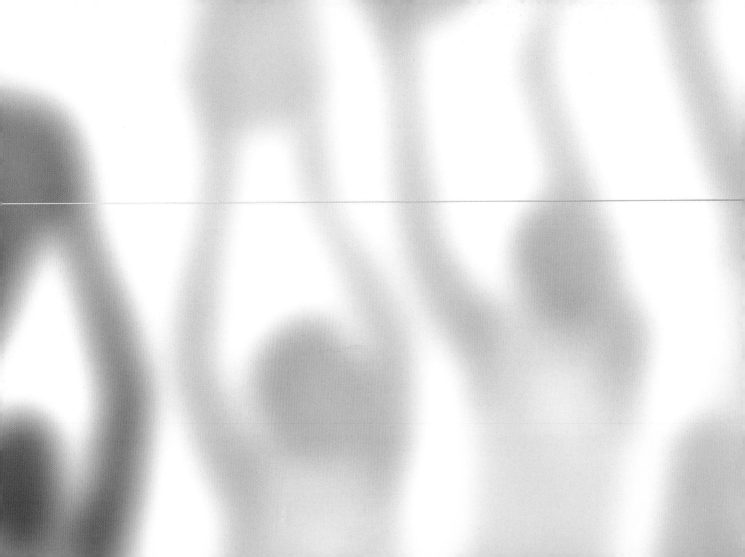

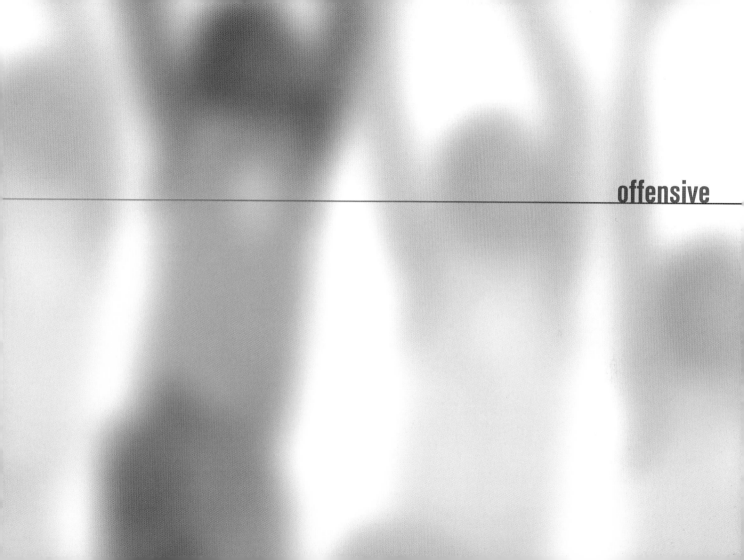

offensive

spin back, forward pivot

Correct footwork is one of the most important and basic skills to master. The simple pivot move demonstrated here will be useful in many game situations.

● With your back to basket, spin the ball out in front of you, using reverse spin.

● As the ball bounces and rebounds back to you, step toward it and then catch it.

● Secure the ball in both hands in the triple-threat position. With your knees flexed, begin the pivot move.

● Make a front (or forward) pivot on your left foot by bringing your right foot forward and around in a counterclockwise direction.

● Your body should turn too as your right foot comes around. Keep your eyes up and note how the ball is positioned to assume the triple threat.

● Bring your right foot around fully and drop it slightly in front of your left foot.

● You should now be facing the basket in the triple-threat position, on balance.

pivot ▶ **turn body** ▶ **balance** ∎

spin back, reverse pivot

The reverse pivot is carried out in the same way as the forward pivot, except that the right foot moves the other way. Both pivots achieve the same result.

● With your back to basket, spin the ball out in front of you, using reverse spin.

● As the ball bounces, step toward it and as it rebounds back toward you, catch it.

● Secure the ball in both hands in the triple-threat position. With knees flexed, begin the pivot move.

● Make a reverse pivot on your left foot by bringing the right foot back and around in a clockwise direction.

● Your body should turn as your right foot comes around. Keep your eyes up and note how the ball is positioned to assume the triple threat.

● Bring your right foot around fully and drop it slightly in front of your left foot.

● You should now be facing the basket in the triple-threat position, on balance.

pivot ▶ **turn body** ▶ **balance** ■

basic dribble

Also known as the "control dribble," this is the one move you are most likely to use in a game.

Practice it using both hands—you will need to be equally skilled with both.

- Keep your head and eyes up at all times while dribbling. Keep your weight evenly distributed and your knees slightly bent.

- Protect the ball by keeping it slightly to one side of your body. Dribble from about waist height, keeping the ball slightly in front of you.

- Extending the elbow and snapping the wrist allows you to bounce the ball on the floor with the required amount of control.

- Keep the ball in your fingers, not on the palm of your hand. As you dribble, move forward on balance. Keep your non-dribbling arm up and out in front of you so as to protect the ball further.

● Note the follow-through of the arm, wrist, and fingers. The body remains balanced and the head and eyes are up.

● The hand goes down to meet the ball shortly after it bounces back off the floor. The force is absorbed back into the arm by bending your elbow.

● Repeat the motion again. What you do at the end of your dribble is dependent upon the game situation.

● Here, the player has come to a one-count stop, on balance, and is ready to assume the triple-threat position.

follow through   **bend the elbow** ▶   ▶   **repeat**   ▶   ■

crossover dribble

The ability to beat the player who is guarding you is an essential skill. Not only must you be able to do this when you do not have the ball, but also when you are in possession of it and dribbling. This is one move that can help you get past a defender.

● Having been in the triple-threat position to assess the game situation, you have decided to dribble. Begin to approach a defender, protecting your dribble by keeping the ball slightly to your side (the right side above).

● As you approach the point at which you want to make your crossover dribble, make a dribble and a body move to your right while getting into a slightly lower body position.

● With the defender now shifting his weight to guard you to your right, you can now begin to elude him by quickly coming to your left.

begin approach ▶ move right ▶ shift quickly left ▶

● Execute the crossover dribble by switching the ball quickly from your right to your left hand, keeping low to the floor. Keep your head and eyes up throughout.

● The crossover dribble should be made using one bounce of the ball from right to left (in this example) and below knee height.

● As you move the ball across your body from right to left, your right foot will also come across, protecting the ball further from the defender, who is now recovering.

● The move should culminate in a change of speed and direction to take you to your left and away from the chasing defender.

switch hands ▶ **protect the ball** **change speed and direction** ■

behind-the-back dribble

Moving the ball behind your back is a dribble move to help you to go past a defender who is guarding you closely. This is an advanced skill, and a very effective one.

● Approach the defender using a standard or controlled dribble. Here, the player is dribbling with his right hand.

● At the point where the defender lunges in to try to steal the ball, begin your maneuver.

● While keeping head and eyes up at all times, begin to angle the next bounce of the ball around your back. Do not "carry" the ball.

● The motion must be continuous. As your arm and the ball are wrapped around behind your back, your body will begin to change direction slightly from right to left.

● The ball is brought around the back completely and is now on the left side of your body.

● Resume your dribble with your left hand.

● Note how the player has also changed direction.

change direction ▶ **bring ball around back** ▶ **resume dribble** ▶ ■

chest pass

The chest pass is the most commonly used pass in the game. Accuracy is the key here, achieved by using good follow-through and keeping eye contact with your intended receiver.

● The pass can be made after a dribble comes to an end.

● From the dribble stance, gather the ball into both your hands, held out in front of your body.

● Spread your fingers around the ball, with your thumbs behind it.

● Begin the pass from around chest height and step forward into the passing action.

● Extend your elbows and snap the wrists to release the ball in a straight line from your chest area to your receiver's chest area.

● Remember to follow through correctly—your arms should finish out in front of your body.

● As the wrists and fingers snap, the backs of your hands will end up facing each other, the palms facing outward.

step forward ▶ **snap wrists** ▶ ▶ **follow through** ‖ ▶ ■

bounce pass

The bounce pass is an invaluable move and can be used in a number of different game situations.

It is very effective after faking another pass, for example an overhead pass.

- The bounce pass can be made after terminating a dribble.

- Gather the ball from the dribble stance into both hands, which are held out in front of your body.

- Spread your fingers around the ball, with your thumbs behind it.

- Begin the pass from around chest height and step forward into the passing action.

● Extend your elbows and snap your wrists to release the ball and direct it at the floor.

● Aim for the ball to bounce just over halfway between passer and receiver.

● The receiver should be able to catch the ball comfortably at around waist height.

● The receiver grips the ball firmly in both hands and brings it up level with his chin.

overhead pass

The overhead pass can be used in a variety of game situations when the angle and trajectory you need to get the ball to the receiver calls for a slightly elevated release.

● As always, start your move from the triple-threat position so that you can assess the game situation and decide on the best response.

● Begin by raising the ball with both hands, knees slightly bent.

● Lift the ball to a position slightly above and in front of the forehead.

● Your hands should be on the sides of the ball, slightly behind the midway point, for maximum control.

● Start to extend your arms, taking a forward step as you do so.

● Straighten your arms and snap your wrists to release the ball.

● Remember always to complete the follow-through.

▶ **step forward** ▶ **snap wrists** ▶ **complete follow-through** ■

baseball pass

When you need to pass over longer distances that would otherwise be reached using a chest or bounce pass, execute the baseball pass.

● From a good power-base of the triple-threat position, with bent knees and a lowered center of gravity, begin to take the ball back with both hands.

● Take the ball back past your ear and transfer your weight from the back foot through to the front foot.

● With the ball still in your hands, your weight shifts from back to front, and your arms begin to come through and forward.

● Keep your (weak) non-passing hand on the ball for as long as possible prior to the release of the ball.

● This is in case you have to adjust and change your decision to throw the baseball pass, depending on how you read the game situation.

● The action of releasing the ball is similar to that of throwing a baseball or a javelin. Your weight now comes through powerfully onto your front foot as your body and arms follow through from behind the ball.

● Project the ball in a straight line toward your intended target. Follow through with the throwing arm in the direction of the flight of the ball.

keep hold of ball ▶ **read the game situation** **release the ball** ▶ ■

receiving

offensive

Receiving the ball is a vital skill that can be practiced and polished in the same way as any other maneuver. Remember that a good pass can be wasted if you are not fully prepared to receive the ball.

● Always be ready to receive a pass. Be alert at all times, with your eyes up and your hands up and out in front of your body.

● To receive a pass, make eye contact with the passer and make an audible and visual signal. For instance, call out your team-mate's name and indicate with your hands where to make the pass.

● Present a target for the ball, with arms extended and fingers spread. This is known as "to show ten," which means all ten fingers are up and showing to the passer and the ball.

■   ▶   **be alert**   ▶   **signal**   ▶   **"show ten"**

● As you are about to catch the ball, make a "nest" for it. When you have caught the ball, wrap your fingers around it to grip it securely.

● At the same time, bend your elbows so you can bring your hands and the ball in toward your body (chest area) to secure and protect it.

● "Look the ball into your hands" is a useful phrase to help you remember how to catch the ball properly.

● As soon as you have caught the ball, get into the triple-threat position, ready to react and make your next appropriate move according to the game situation.

v-cut

In basketball, the V-cut is a basic way of getting free, or open, for a pass. This is a simple method to use against a defensive player at any level of the game, and it relies on a quick change of speed and direction.

● Maintain good balance throughout and begin by taking your defender one way. Above, the player is first going toward his left.

● This first move can be made at a relatively slow pace as you are simply trying to outwit and outmaneuver your opponent.

● By planting your left foot, the all-important change of speed and direction can now take place.

● Now, push off your left foot and make a hard and sharp cut in the opposite direction.

● The shape of the letter "V" is transcribed on the floor, and you have now eluded your defender by putting him off balance.

● With the change of direction, you should—if all has gone well—be free for the pass.

● Having executed the V-cut, you are now free to signal for the ball and carry on according to the game situation.

right-hand lay up

The right-hand lay up is the most fundamental of shots and the one resulting in the highest percentage of scores. All players must be able to execute this shot using the correct hand movements and footwork.

● Begin the approach to basket on the right side, using your right hand to dribble the ball. Keep the ball protected from the defense.

● Keep your head up and your eyes focused on the target.

● As you approach the three-second lane, begin to finish your dribble while still protecting the ball on the right side of your body.

protect the ball ▶ focus on target ▶ finish dribble

● Step first onto your right foot. At the same time, move the ball up to the shooting position above the right shoulder.

● The next step is with your left foot. Keep your eyes focused on the target and raise the ball above your right shoulder.

● Use your two steps to get you as near to the basket as possible. Jump off your left foot, as high as you can, up toward the basket to release the ball.

● Extend your elbow and snap the wrist of your (right) shooting arm and hand to shoot the ball softly off the backboard. Aim for the top corner of the small black square on the right side of the rim.

▶   **raise ball**   ❚❚   **release the ball**   ▶   ◼

left-hand lay up

Even if you are right handed, there will be times when you will need to approach the basket on the left side of the court. Therefore, you must be able to execute a left-handed lay up using the correct footwork. As with every other skill, the only path to success is practice, practice, practice.

● Begin the approach to basket on the left side, using your left hand to dribble the ball. Keep the ball protected from the defense.

● Keep your head up and your eyes focused on the target.

● As you approach the three-second lane, begin to terminate your dribble while still protecting the ball on the left side of your body.

● Step first onto your left foot. At the same time, move the ball up to the shooting position above the left shoulder.

● The next step will be with your right foot. Keep your eyes focused on the target and extend the ball above the left shoulder.

● Use your two steps to get you as near to the basket as possible. Jump off your right foot, as high as you can, up toward the basket to release the ball.

● Extend the elbow and snap the wrist of your (left) shooting arm and hand to shoot the ball softly off the backboard. Aim for the top corner of the small black square on the left side of the rim.

move ball to shooting position   ❚❚   ▶   **release the ball**   ◼

power lay up right to left

This move is made when you have a path to the basket but there is a defender on your right and one on your left when you arrive at the basket. You have to be strong and determined now in order to achieve the shot. You might also be able to draw a foul for a bonus-free throw.

● Make your dribble approach from the right side of the lane while keeping your head up and your eyes on the target. Keep the ball protected on your right side. You will be power-dribbling your way to the basket.

● Try to find a gap on the floor as near to the basket as possible (very often in between two defenders). Finish your dribble and be ready to come to a two-footed, one-count stop while protecting the ball.

● You have now gone across the lane and to the left side of the basket.

■　　　　　　　▶　　**power dribble**　　　▶　　**finish dribble**　　　▶

● With elbows out, ball at chin height, and knees bent, plant both feet at the same time, ready to "explode," and jump off both feet.

● Before leaving the floor to jump toward the basket, execute a "pump fake," which is basically a type of "shot fake" made by slightly raising the ball and your head and shoulders up toward the basket.

● This makes defenders jump into the air in an attempt to block the (assumed) shot. Then, jump up straight and high, protecting the ball, and shoot the ball off the backboard into the basket on the left side of the rim.

● Maintain your balance throughout, as you may get fouled during the shot or you may need to go back up for a rebound if you miss the shot.

get ready to jump ❙❙ ▶ **execute "pump fake"** **jump and shoot** ▶ ■

left-hand reverse lay up

There will be times in a game when your usual path to basket for a right-handed lay up on the right-hand side of the basket will be blocked by a defensive player or players. You should be able to avoid the charging foul and go across and underneath the rim to lay the ball up on the other side.

● From the triple-threat position, begin your normal approach to the basket for a right-hand lay up on the right side.

● Dribble with the right hand, making sure to protect the ball as you go.

● Upon picking up the dribble, begin your normal footwork for a right-hand lay up. Keep up a right-foot/left-foot rhythm.

● Instead of going to the right side of the rim, travel across and underneath the basket, now protecting the ball on the left side of your body.

● Jump up on the left side of the rim and shoot the lay up off the backboard on that side with your left hand.

● Try to release the ball from as close to the rim and backboard as possible, using the rim as a "shield" for the ball so that the shot cannot be blocked.

● Sometimes, the reverse lay up can be finished using the right hand on the left side of the rim, releasing it with a back-flip of the wrist.

protect the ball, left side   ▶   shoot   ▶   shield   ▶   ■

jump shot

This is the most commonly used shot in the game of basketball. Regular practice using the correct techniques is the key to becoming a successful jump shooter and to acquiring and maintaining a good shooting percentage. You have to work at it.

● From the triple-threat position, which means having a good base of support and good body balance, start to flex your ankles and knees, ready to jump.

● Keep your eyes focused on the target (the back of the rim). Your feet are pointing at the target. For a right-handed shooter, the right foot is slightly ahead of the left. Your shoulders are facing the target.

● Bring the ball up to the shooting position (slightly in front of, and above, your forehead). At the same time, your lower body is getting ready to jump straight up into the air.

● The elbow of your shooting hand (right in the picture above) is now also pointing at the target. Your wrist is "cocked" and the ball is on the soft pads of the tops of your fingers, ready for the release.

● Jump into the air, keeping your body straight. At the top of the jump, begin to release the ball by extending your elbow and snapping your wrist. The non-shooting hand (left in the picture above) is not used in the shot.

● The ball is released upward and forward in a high arc toward the basket. Follow through by straightening your shooting arm and snapping your wrist and fingers. Keep your head still and your eyes focussed on the target.

● Land in the same spot from which you took off. Maintain your follow-through even after the ball has left your hand. Land and keep your balance, ready to react to the next game situation.

jump hook

There will be times when you find yourself very close to the basket but without much room to move left or right for a lay up. The jump hook is a useful shot in this situation and is also a difficult technique for defenders to block.

- Approach the basket using a one- or two-bounce dribble.

- With eyes up, locating the target, come to a good, strong, one-count stop, on balance.

- Your feet are almost parallel with the backboard and the ball is protected in both hands, with your elbows out. Keep your knees flexed.

■ ▶ **one-count stop** ❙❙ ▶ **protect ball**

● Move suddenly upward off your left foot while pushing the ball upward through the mid-line of the body. Note that your left elbow is leading the way.

● As you jump, continue to lift the ball upward to the shooting position, which will be high above your head.

● Your body position is almost sideways on to the basket. You should now be sighting the target over your left shoulder.

● Release the ball at the top of the jump with a "hooking" motion of the shooting wrist and hand. Follow through and try to land in the same spot that you took off from.

lead with elbow ❙❙ ▶ **be sideways on** ▶ **follow through** ◾

shot fake & drive

This demonstrates a way of moving that will enable you to beat your defender and create scoring opportunities for you and your team-mates.

● Provided you are within your shooting range, with the defender in front of you, begin to make a shot fake from the triple-threat position.

● The shot fake is a motion with the arms, shoulders, and ball that should look identical to your jump-shot technique, except that you do not complete the move and release the ball.

● You are simply trying to get your defender to react to the threat and potential of your jump shot.

● Many defenders will actually leave the floor and jump in an attempt to block the (assumed) shot.

● At this point, bring the ball back down and protect it on the outside hip (right in the sequence above).

● Begin to drive past the now off-balance defender. Protect the ball and have your head up and your eyes on the target.

● If the game situation dictates, then continue your drive to the basket and take the lay-up shot.

jab fake & go

The aim of this offensive move is to enable you to elude and beat a defender who is guarding you closely.

● From the triple-threat position, you now know the position of your defender.

● With the right foot, make a jab step to your right (the defender's left). While executing this move, bring the ball onto your right hip in order to protect it.

● The action of the jab step must be made quickly while maintaining balance. The defender is guarding you closely and your aim is to step just past his left foot.

● At the same time, try to get your head and shoulders just past the defender's left hip.

● At this point, you have him beaten. Now, dribble the ball and lift your back (left) foot and continue past him.

● Once past the defender, you can assess the game situation and make a decision to continue to drive to basket, pass, or shoot.

● In the instance shown above, the player has decided to pass to an open team-mate.

get past defender ▶ dribble assess game situation ‖ ▶ ■

shot fake, one dribble, & jump shot

This is another good move to make to try to beat an opponent who is closely guarding you. Assume that you have the ball and are away from the basket.

● Provided you are within your shooting range, with the defender in front of you, begin to make a shot fake from the triple-threat position.

● The shot fake is a motion with the arms, shoulders, and ball, which should look identical to your jump-shot technique, except that you do not complete the move and release the ball.

● You are simply trying to get your defender to react to the threat and potential of your jump shot. Many defenders will actually leave the floor and jump in an attempt to block the (assumed) shot.

● At this point, bring the ball back down and protect it on the outside hip (right in the picture above).

● Begin to drive past the defender, who is now off balance. Protect the ball and have your head up and your eyes on the target.

● Make one dribble to your right. This should be enough to put some distance between you and the defender, who is now recovering.

● Go up and take your jump shot, concentrating, as always, on achieving perfect form.

drop step baseline

This move for a post player is a very useful one if the defender is playing you slightly to the topside, that is, nearer the free throw line. You can either detect that he is already there, or you can try to make him move a little in that direction by executing a fake.

● Having caught the ball in the low post and located the position of the defensive player, the offensive player makes a ball fake to the inside, that is, the opposite way to the move he actually intends to make.

● The offensive player does not need to move his feet: he simply brings the ball, and his head and shoulders, to the right in a quick fake move. The aim is to make the defender shift slightly to the right.

● The offensive player now lifts and steps on his left foot, pointing it across the defender toward the basket.

● Keeping the ball protected as he does so, the defender is now pinned behind the attacker. The offensive player can dribble the ball using a power dribble or crab dribble.

● This involves the offensive player taking one hard bounce between his feet, which are now well spread out.

● After this dribble, he collects the ball, gets his elbows out to protect it, keeps his shoulders parallel with the end line and backboard, and jumps up to power the ball into the basket.

● The offensive player should try to land where he took off from, in case he needs to go back up and rebound a missed shot.

pin defender behind ▶ **one hard bounce** ▶ **shoot** ▶ ■

drop step middle

The ability to elude your defender in the low post area with a variety of moves is a useful addition to your whole game. This move ends with a point-blank shot at the basket from the middle of the lane.

● In the post-up situation, protect the ball and locate the position of your defender.

● Try to get the defender off balance by faking him in the opposite direction to your eventual move.

● Make a head and shoulders fake toward the baseline side. Keep both feet still. If the defender moves this way (thinking that you are going that way), move in the opposite direction.

● Now, come back the opposite way, ie, toward the free-throw line. Lift off the right foot and direct it toward the middle of the three-second lane.

● At the same time, make a power dribble between your feet to gain further ground in the direction of the basket area. The defender should now be "locked off" behind you.

● Now, you can bring both feet and the ball around to face the basket. Be sure to protect the ball.

● Keeping your elbows out and your knees bent, begin your shot toward the basket. You may need to precede the shot with a pump fake.

● Go up strong and power the ball into the basket. Try to land in the same spot that you took off from.

power inside ▶ **protect the ball** ▶ **shoot** ❙❙ ▶ ■

inside pivot, & shoot

offensive

If you are playing in the low-post position, you will need a variety of moves. Your choice depends on where your defender is playing you. The inside pivot & shoot is just one move you can try. Make sure that you can easily locate the basket after having pivoted to face it.

● Having received the ball in the low post, make sure you protect it and locate the position of your defender.

● If the defender is playing directly behind and slightly off your position, then, with a quick inside turn, you can momentarily "freeze" him and get a shot off.

● Protect the ball by keeping it at chin height and your elbows up and out.

<m

● Pivot on your right foot as shown, lifting your left foot up off the floor as you swing it across your right leg.

● This brings your body around to face the basket. Your left elbow has cleared a little amount of space for you to get into the shooting position.

● As your left foot is swung back and planted slightly behind your right foot, jump and shoot in one motion.

● Try to take off and land in the same spot, following through and remaining on balance so that you can react to the next game situation.

pivot on right foot ▶ **get into shooting position** ▶ **jump and shoot** ‖ ▶ ■

screen & roll

offensive

The art of setting a screen to get a team-mate free for a pass is an important strategy in team basketball. In this situation, the rules will allow a certain amount of contact to be made between two opposing players.

● First, you must have located the position of your team-mate and his defender.

● Now, make an approach with the aim of making contact with the defender's inside shoulder (that is, the shoulder nearest the midline of the court).

● You must arrive at a point on the floor so that, at the moment of contact with your opponent, you are stationary. Have your knees bent, your back straight, and head up with a good strong base of support.

■   ▶   locate teammate   ▶   approach to make contact   ‖   ▶

● Make a "double arm bar," as shown, with your forearms held out in front of your body. It is up to your team-mate—whom you are screening for—to maneuver the defender into your screen.

● Sometimes, there can be a lot of body contact, so the body positioning described is essential to avoid injury. The impact can be absorbed, momentarily, by the arms when held as shown.

● After contact has occurred (assuming that the screen has been successful in freeing up your team-mate), the screening player should roll toward the ball (and very often the basket too).

● To execute this roll, make a reverse pivot on your left foot, locate the ball, and, if appropriate, signal to receive it.

make "double arm bar" ▶   **absorb impact** ❙❙ ▶   **roll towards ball** ▶   ■

using a screen topside

This is another way of using a screen that has been set for you by a team-mate away from the ball.

This time the defender plays behind the screen, so you need to execute a topside cut.

● Begin to use the screen by making a V-cut. Above, you can see the player going first left and then coming back, to his right.

● Having read the position of your defensive player, start to execute the required cut, which will be the topside cut off the screen.

● Quickly change direction by pushing off your left foot to elude your defensive player.

● Couple your change of direction with a change of speed as your move takes you in front of the screen and toward the ball. This is the topside cut.

■ ▶ **execute topside cut** ▶ **change direction** ‖ ▶ **change speed**

● Once you have made the topside cut, look to receive the pass by signaling, visually and audibly, to the passer.

● Catch the ball and get yourself into a potential scoring position.

● If you've executed well, you will have managed to lose your defender by making him go the wrong way and get caught on the screen.

● Having caught the ball, pivot to face the basket in the triple-threat position and be ready to go up for a jump shot.

using a screen—backcut

This is another way of using a screen set for you by a teammate away from the ball. The one you opt for will be decided by the position of the defensive player. If your defensive player plays "on topside" of the screen, then you will need to execute the backcut or "backdoor" cut shown here.

● Begin to use the screen by first stepping up as if to use it by cutting topside of it toward the ball.

● Having read the position of your defensive player, begin to execute the required cut, which will be the backcut off the screen.

● Quickly change direction by pushing off your right foot to elude your defensive player.

● Couple your change of direction with a change of speed as your move takes you behind the screen and toward the basket. This is the backcut or "backdoor" cut.

● Once you have made the backcut, look to receive the pass by signaling, visually and audibly, to the passer.

● Catch the ball at the end of your backcut to get yourself into a potential scoring position. Hopefully, you have managed to lose your defender by making him go the wrong way and get caught on the screen.

● If the cut is into the basket area and the pass is caught, you are in a good position to go up to the basket for the score.

change speed ▶ signal ‖ ▶ get into scoring position ▶ ■

up-and-under move

This is another "post move." It is an advanced move and an extremely effective one when executed correctly.

● From the post-up position, protect the ball, having made sure that the defender is playing behind you.

● Begin to make a forward or front pivot. Above, the player is pivoting on his right foot.

● With the ball at about chin height, protect it with elbows out and continue your pivot toward the inside of the three-second lane.

● As you complete your front pivot, you will be facing your defender and the basket. Begin your pump fake move.

protect the ball ▶ make a strong pivot

● The pump fake involves raising the ball and your head and shoulders as if you were going to shoot the ball.

● The aim of this maneuver is to get the defender to anticipate a shot and react, perhaps by jumping to attempt to block the shot.

● Don't release the ball. Instead, bring it down onto the outside hip and, at the same time, step "under" and across the airborne defender with the left foot.

● The step through is directed toward the basket, and you can dribble the ball once you get all the way to the basket for the shot and release.

jab, cross over, & go

This is another move in a series of one-on-one moves that is useful to you when faced with trying to beat your defensive player. First, get the defender off balance by using the jab fake.

● From the triple-threat position, begin the move by making a jab step (on the right foot, above). This jab step is a fake but needs to look to the defender as if you intend to go to the right.

● As you make the jab step, bring the ball down and protect it on the outside hip. At this point, if the defender has reacted by shifting to his left, you have him where you want him.

● Swing your right foot across your body, right to left, placing your right foot to the right of the defender. At the same time, swing the ball through onto the left hip.

● This is the cross-over move, and the idea is to "lock" the defender's feet behind your front foot (right).

● Having now got the defender off balance, you have, in fact, changed direction and are now able to go on the dribble to your left.

● Keeping your body between the defender and the ball, dribble now with your left hand to go past, and beat, the recovering defender.

● React to the game situation. In the sequence above, the player has driven all the way to the basket.

defensive

blocking out

Most contact in basketball will result in a foul being called by the officials. However, this is one area of the game where the rules allow a certain amount of contact. When a shot goes up and you are the defensive player, you should try to "box out" or "block out" in an effort to prevent your opponent from getting the rebound.

● As the shot goes up, make sure you can locate the player you are guarding.

● Step toward this player and make contact, as shown above, by using the legal "arm bar."

● Your opponent will try to get around you in an attempt to go after the rebounding ball. So, start to pivot to block his intended path.

● Above, the offensive player is moving to his left. Immediately, make a reverse pivot on your right foot in order to block the way.

● If possible, contact should be maintained and this is still within the rules. Try now to locate the rebounding ball while at the same time adopting the "box-out" position.

● With your hands up and your elbows up and out, bend your knees and try to "pin" your opponent using your lower back and lower body. This contact is maintained for a second or two at most in any rebound situation.

● After blocking out or boxing out your opponent, go for the rebound and try to secure the ball and the possession for your team.

maintain contact   ‖   ▶   pin your opponent

defensive stance & lateral slide

The ability to react and move quickly is essential to being a good defensive player. You have to be able to guard opponents in all game situations, and the most efficient way is to stay down in the defensive stance and move your feet in the appropriate manner.

● In this defensive stance, the player's feet are about shoulder-width apart, backside is down, back is straight, head is up, and hands are up and active. One heel should be roughly in line with the toes of the other foot.

● In order to move laterally, try to make foot movements that involve a step-slide action. As you stay down low, the center of gravity remains constant,

● Move your feet quickly, trying to maintain contact with the floor fas much as you possibly can.

● As you move your feet, your body weight should remain slightly on the balls of your feet.

● Your feet should not be brought together, as this raises the center of gravity of the body and throws you off balance.

● Step and slide to the left by turning your left foot slightly outward in the direction you want to slide.

● As you now want to change direction and come back toward the right, push off the left foot and step-slide, with your right foot leading.

● The position of the hands and arms will change, usually depending on what the player you are guarding is doing with the ball.

forward slide with close out

When defending the player with the ball, it may be that he dribbles backward at some point and/or catches the ball and is ready to take a shot. Depending on your court position at that moment, you will need to be able to execute a movement that takes you toward your opponent—without fouling or being off balance—in order to contest the shot.

● In the defensive stance, begin to move forward by adjusting the position of your feet and shifting the body from left to right (or vice versa).

● Once again, use the step-slide movement of your feet to take you forward and to the left, then forward again and to the right.

● You will need to adjust your feet and body position according to what your opponent is doing.

● If the attacker elects to shoot the jump shot, recognize this and begin to bring a hand and foot forward, ready to contest and put pressure on the shot. Above, the player is bringing his left foot and left hand forward.

● Get a hand up in order to try to distract the shooter (or, even, to attempt to block the shot).

● Do not jump into the air at this point unless your opponent has already used and picked up his dribble. This action of bringing the hand and foot forward is known as "closing out."

● After closing out on the shot, you will probably need to block out (or box out) the shooter. Locate the player, make a pivot into the path of that player, and make contact in order to block out this potential rebounder.

apply pressure   ▶   distract or block   ‖   ▶   close out   ▶   ■

backward slide & dead dribble

The ability to keep an offensive player who is dribbling the ball in front of you and apply the right pressure on the ball when he or she picks up the dribble is the key to effective defense.

● In a balanced, defensive stance, the weight is slightly on the balls of the feet, the hands are up and active, and the feet are "alive" and responsive. Be alert and ready to react quickly to the ball-handler's movements.

● Keeping your back straight and your head up, begin moving your feet in a step-slide motion left and right, keeping the dribbler in front of you. Try to keep an arm's-length distance between you and the offensive player.

● Without lunging in, which will put you off balance, keep your hands active, ready to jab at the ball when your opponent is off guard. While retreating, try to prevent the ball-handler getting past you.

● If the dribbler picks up the dribble, start repositioning yourself forward, toward your opponent. With knees slightly flexed, get as close as you can without making contact, yelling "Dead! Dead!"

● This tells your team-mates that the dribble has been picked up and you are covering it. With your hands fairly close together, start to "mirror" the ball with both hands.

● This means "tracing" the movement of the ball as the offensive player tries to pass or shoot it. Be careful not to foul, keep your hands in the same plane as your body, and apply maximum pressure to your opponent.

● Try to force a five-second violation through your pressure on the ball. Be ready to react again, depending on the movement of the ball and the player you are guarding.

▶ **reposition forward** **"mirror" the ball** ▶ **apply maximum pressure** ▶

defensive rebound & outlet pass

Rebounding is a crucial part of the defensive game. The success of this move means you will gain extra possession for your team, which could make all the difference between winning and losing. Get after it!

● Having watched the flight of the ball and boxed out the player you were guarding, establish your rebound position.

● Create a good base of support by keeping your feet approximately shoulder-width apart, knees bent, and back straight. Have your arms up, ready to go and catch the ball.

● Keep your eyes focused on where the ball will rebound from. Jump as high as you can and try to extend your arms toward the ball.

● Try to catch the ball at the top of your jump with both hands.

● As you land, try to maintain your balance. Bring the ball down no lower than chin height and keep your elbows out. This helps to protect the ball from opponents. Grip the ball firmly with both hands.

● Protect the ball and begin to pivot away from the basket, out toward the sideline—on the same side of the basket as you rebounded the ball.

● Locate an open team-mate for a good outlet pass. This could be a chest, bounce, or overhead pass.

maintain balance ‖ ▶ **pivot away from basket** ▶ ■

deny the wing & back door

If you are guarding a player who is one pass away from the ball, you should try to "deny" the ball; that is, stop your opponent from receiving it. In the sequence below, imagine you are the player in green.

● The defensive player has his arm nearest the ball extended and up in the passing lane, his palm toward the ball, and left foot forward and up toward the midcourt corner. He "looks" a little over his left shoulder.

● The defensive player will be making a series of step-slide movements, defensively sliding back and forth to deny the offensive player the ball. The offensive player will be trying to get free to receive it.

● The defender's denial motion here is similar to a fencer moving forward. He tries to maintain about one arm's-length distance between himself and his opponent. Also, he should be slightly back toward his basket.

● If the offensive player starts to try to cut backdoor or make a backcut, the defender quickly adjusts his feet and brings his other hand (right in the picture) up to deny the offensive player once again.

● At the same time, the defender quickly turns his head so that he is now "looking" over his right shoulder.

● He now has to make a couple of step-slide movements in the opposite direction, in order to try to deny the ball to his opponent.

● The defender must regain vision of the ball and his opponent (through peripheral vision) as quickly as possible. Also, he must maintain a constant stance as this allows him to react and move quickly and efficiently.

● The defensive player's position in relation to his opponent and the ball is now the same as at the start. For the moment, though, his position in relation to his defensive basket has changed.

step-slide, opposite way   **maintain stance**

denial defense & helpside position

This move helps you stop a player who is one pass away from the ball from getting it. The player below is guarding a player on the right side of the court in the "wing" area between the lane and the sideline.

● In the defensive stance, your arm nearest the ball is extended and up in the passing lane, palm facing the ball. Your right foot is forward, facing the midcourt corner. Your head is turned a little over your right shoulder.

● Make a series of step-slide movements, defensively sliding back and forth so as to deny the offensive player the ball (the offensive player will of course be trying to get free to receive it).

● If the offensive player starts to try to cut backdoor or make a backcut toward the basket, adjust your feet and bring your other hand (left, above) up to deny the attacker once again.

● At the same time, turn your head quickly to look over your left shoulder. You will now have to make a couple of step-slide movements in the opposite direction, in order to try to deny the offensive player the ball.

■　▶　**step-slide**　▶　**deny again**　⏸　▶　**step-slide, opposite way**

● As the offensive player has now cut into the three-second area, he must exit within that time allocation. Above, imagine he is going to cut across the basket and out of the lane on the other side of the court.

● Having denied the offensive player with your left arm up, you can see that he is going out and away from the ball.

● Begin to pivot to reposition yourself according to the position of the offensive player and the ball. Make a reverse pivot on your left foot, and maintain your balance and defensive stance.

● Regain peripheral vision of the ball and your opponent. With arms up, you are now in the helpside position in the middle of the lane area, in defensive stance, "pointing" to the player you are guarding and to the ball.

index

FIBA 8–9, 12
fitness 8, 14–15
five-second violation 87
flow sequences, understanding 19
follow-through
    dribbling 27
    passing 32, 33
    shooting 53
forward pivot 22–23, 74

forward slide 84–85
forwards 10–11
fouls 8–9, 48, 49
freezing defenders 66

G
glutes stretch 18
governing bodies 6, 12
guards 10–11

H
hamstring stretch 18
hands
    defending 82–83, 85, 86
    dribbling 26–27
    passing 32–33, 37, 38–39
    receiving passes 40–41
    shooting 45, 51, 53
health 14
helpside position 93
history 6–7
hook shot 54–55

I
inside pivot & shoot 66–67
inverted hurdler's stretch 16

J
jab, cross over & go 76–77
jab fake & go 58–59
jump hook 54–55
jump shot 52–53

L
lateral slides 82–83
lay up
    left-hand 46–47
    left-hand reverse 50–51
    power right to left 48–49
    right-hand 44–45
left-hand dribbling 26
left-hand lay up 46–47, 50–51
left-hand reverse lay up 50–51
locking defenders feet 77
long distance pass 38–39
low post area 62–67
lower back stretch 18

M
"mirror" ball movements 87

N
Naismith, Dr James 6–7
National Basketball Association
    (NBA) 6, 8–9, 12
NCAA 8–9, 12

O
offensive moves
    combinations 56–65, 74–77
    dribbling 26–31, 63, 65
    fakes 56–65, 74–77
    passing 32–41
    pivots 22–25, 66–67, 69, 74
    screening 68–73
    shooting 44–55
    v-cut 42–43

Olympic Games 6, 7
outdoor courts 13
overhead pass 36–37

P
passes
    baseball pass 38–39
    bounce pass 34–35
    chest pass 32–33
    outlet pass 89
    overhead pass 36–37
    receiving 40–41, 70–73
pivot moves 22–25, 66–67, 69, 74
player positions 10–11
post area 62–67, 74–75
post-up position 74
power dribble 63, 65
power lay up right to left 48–49
pretzel stretch 16
protecting ball 57, 61, 66, 74, 89
pump fake 49, 75

Q
quadriceps stretch 17

R
rebounding ball 11, 80–81, 85, 88–89
receiving passes 40–41, 70–73
reverse pivot 24–25, 69
right-hand lay up 44–45
roll move 69
rules 8–9